I0117370

George Daniels

The Chicago & Pacific Railroad

A description of the new railroad line across the state of Illinois

George Daniels

The Chicago & Pacific Railroad
A description of the new railroad line across the state of Illinois

ISBN/EAN: 9783337257675

Printed in Europe, USA, Canada, Australia, Japan

Cover: Foto ©Andreas Hilbeck / pixelio.de

More available books at **www.hansebooks.com**

THE

CHICAGO & PACIFIC

RAILROAD,

A DESCRIPTION OF

THE NEW RAILROAD LINE

ACROSS THE STATE OF ILLINOIS,

FROM

CHICAGO TO THE MISSISSIPPI RIVER,

WITH COPY OF CHARTER, MAPS, ETC.

COMPILED BY

GEORGE H. DANIELS.

CHICAGO, MAY 1, 1873.

KNIGHT & LEONARD, PRINTERS, 105-109 MADISON ST., CHICAGO.

THE

CHICAGO & PACIFIC

RAILROAD COMPANY.

DIRECTORS.

THOMAS S. DOBBINS, ROSELLE M. HOUGH,

GEORGE S. BOWEN, WALTER L. PEASE,

GEORGE YOUNGS, JOHN S. WILCOX,

WILLIAM B. HOWARD.

OFFICERS.

THOMAS S. DOBBINS, *President.*

GEORGE S. BOWEN, *Vice-Prest. and Treasurer.*

WILLIAM T. HUGHES, *Secretary.*

JOHN S. WILCOX, *Solicitor.*

JAMES M. WHITMAN, *Chief Engineer.*

JAMES K. LAKE, *Superintendent.*

I. G. OGDEN, JR., *Auditor and Paymaster.*

GEORGE H. DANIELS, *Gen'l Pass. and Freight Agt.*

THE CHARTER

OF THE

ATLANTIC AND PACIFIC RAILROAD COMPANY.

AN ACT TO INCORPORATE THE ATLANTIC AND PACIFIC RAILROAD COMPANY.

SECTION 1. *Be it enacted by the people of the State of Illinois, represented in the General Assembly,* That John V. Ayer, Darwin Harvey, Elliott Anthony, and Azariah T. Galt, and their associates, successors, heirs, and assigns, are hereby created a body politic and corporate, by the name and style of the "Atlantic and Pacific Railroad Company," with perpetual succession, and by that name be and are hereby made capable, in law and equity, to sue and be sued, plead and be impleaded, defend and be defended in any court of law and equity in this State, or any other place; to make and use a common seal, and the same to alter or renew at pleasure; and shall be, and are hereby, vested with all powers, privileges, and immunities which are or may be necessary to carry into effect the purposes and objects of this act as hereinafter set forth; and said company is hereby authorized and empowered to locate, construct, and complete a railroad from a line between the States of Indiana and Illinois, at a point in Cook county, Illinois, to be hereafter selected, by the way of the city of Chicago, Ill., to the Mississippi river, at any point at or north of the city of Savanna, to be hereafter located: said railroad to be laid out and constructed upon the most eligible route between the points above named; and for this purpose the said

Corporators.

Name and style.

Powers.

company is authorized to lay out and locate its said road with a six-foot gauge, or otherwise, through the whole length of said route; and, for the purpose of cutting embankments, stone and gravel, may take and appropriate as much more land as may be necessary for the construction and security of said road.

Capital stock.

SEC. 2. The capital stock of said company shall consist of two million dollars, which may be increased to any amount not exceeding the actual estimated cost of constructing and equiping their said road, to be divided into shares of one hundred dollars each. All the corporate powers of said company shall be vested in and exercised by a board of seven directors, who shall be chosen by the stockholders of said company, in the manner hereinafter provided; who shall hold their offices for one year, or until their successors shall be elected and qualified; and said directors, a majority of whom shall form a quorum for the transaction of business, shall elect one of their number to be the president of the company; and said board of directors shall have power to appoint all necessary clerks, secretary, treasurer, and all other officers deemed necessary in the transaction of the business of said company.

Directors.

Surveys of route.

SEC. 3. The said corporation is hereby authorized by its agents, surveyors, and engineers, to cause such examinations and surveys to be made of the ground and the country as shall be necessary to determine the most desirable route whereon to construct their said railroad; and it shall be lawful for said company to enter upon and take possession of and use all such lands and real estate as will or may be necessary for the construction and maintenance of the said railroad, its depots, side-tracks, water-stations, engine-houses, machine-shops, and other buildings and appendages necessary to the construction of said railroad. Provided that all lands or real estate entered upon and taken possession of by said corporation, for the purpose and accommodation of said railroad, or upon which

Lands taken.

the site for said railroad shall have been located or determined by said corporation, shall be paid for by said company, in damages, if any be sustained by the owner or owners thereof, by the use of the same for the purposes of said railroad; and all lands entered upon and taken for use of said corporation which are not donated to said company shall be paid for by said corporation, at such times as may be mutually agreed upon by the said corporation and the owner or owners of such lands; and, in case of disagreement, the price shall be estimated, fixed, and recovered in the manner provided for taking lands for the construction of public roads, canals, or other public works, as prescribed by the act concerning the right of way, approved March 3, 1845, and the amendments thereto.

Annual meetings.

SEC. 4. The time of holding the annual meeting of said directors shall be fixed and determined by the by-laws of said company; and at all meetings each stockholder shall be entitled to a vote in person, or by lawful proxy, one vote for each share of stock, he, she, or they may hold, *bona fide*, in said company, upon which all installments called have been paid.

Books of subscription.

SEC. 5. The persons named in the first section of this act are hereby appointed commissioners, who, or a majority of them, are hereby authorized to open, or cause to be opened, subscription books for the stock of said company, at such time and place as they may think proper; and also to appoint one or more agents to open such books and receive such subscriptions. The said commissioners, or their agents, shall require each subscriber to pay five dollars, or execute a note therefor, as they shall determine, on each share subscribed, at the time of subscribing; and whenever fifty thousand dollars shall be subscribed, the said commissioners shall call a meeting (or a majority of them shall) of the stockholders, by giving twenty days' notice in some newspaper printed in the city of Chicago, or by personal notice, served upon each of the stockholders, of the time and place of such meeting, at least ten days previous to the time of such meeting; and at such meeting, it shall be lawful for the stockholders to elect the directors of said company, and transact any other necessary business; and when the directors are chosen, the said commissioners shall deliver said subscription books, with all sums of money and notes received by them, or by any agent appointed by them as commissioner, to said directors. No person shall be a director unless he shall be a *bona fide* stockholder in said company.

Subscription to stock.

SEC. 6. The directors of said company, after the same is organized, are hereby authorized and empowered to take and receive subscriptions to their said capital stock, on such terms and in such amounts as they may deem for the interest of said company, and as they may prescribe by their by-laws or regulations, from any other railroad or corporation, and from any county, city, town, or village making the same, provided said company shall not be authorized to take or receive subscriptions to its capital stock payable in real estate.

ght of way.

SEC. 7. That the right of way, and the real estate purchased for the right of way, or other purposes, by said company, whether by mutual agreement or otherwise, or which shall become the property of said company by operation of law, as in this act provided, shall, upon payment of the amount of money belonging to the owner or owners of said lands as a compensation for the same, become the property of said company in fee simple.

SEC. 8. The said corporation may take and transport on said railroad any person or persons, merchandise or other property by the force and power of steam, or animals, or any combination of them; and may fix, establish, take, and receive such rates of toll for all passengers and property transported upon the same, as the directors shall from time to time establish; and the directors are hereby authorized and empowered to make all necessary rules, by-laws, regulations, and ordinances that they may deem necessary and expedient to accomplish the designs and purposes, and to carry into effect the provisions of this act, and for the transfer and assignment of its stock, which is hereby declared personal property, and transferable in such manner as shall be provided by the by-laws and ordinances of said company. By-laws.

SEC. 9. In case of death, resignation, or removal of the president, vice-president, or any director, at any time before the annual election, such vacancies shall be filled for the remainder of the year, whenever they may happen, by the board of directors; and in case of absence of the president and vice-president, the board of directors shall have power to appoint a president *pro tempore*, who shall have and exercise such powers and functions as the by-laws of the said corporation may provide. In case it should at any time happen that an election shall not be made on any day on which, in pursuance of this act, it ought to be made, the said corporation shall not, for that cause, be deemed dissolved, but such election shall be held at any other time directed by the by-laws of said corporation. Vacancy.

SEC. 10. Whenever it shall be necessary for the construction of said railroad to intersect or cross a track of any other railroad, or stream of water, or watercourse, or road, or highway, on the route of said railroad, it shall be lawful for the company to construct their railroad across or upon the same, provided the said railroad shall restore the railroad, stream of water, watercourse, road, or highway thus intersected or crossed, to its former state, or in a sufficient manner not materially to impair its usefulness. Crossing of roads.

SEC. 11. Said company shall have power, and it is hereby made lawful for said company to unite or consolidate its railroad with any other railroad or railroads now constructed, or being constructed, or which may hereafter be constructed, within this or any other Consolidation.

State, which may cross or intersect the same, or be built along the line thereof, upon such terms as may be mutually agreed upon between the said company or any other company; and for that purpose full power is hereby given to said company to make and execute such contracts with any other company or companies as will secure the object of such connection or consolidations.

Borrow money. SEC. 12. That the said railroad company, by this act incorporated, shall have power to borrow money on the credit of the company, not exceeding its authorized capital stock, at a rate of interest not exceeding ten per cent. per annum, payable semi-annually; and may execute bonds therefor, with interest coupons thereto annexed, and secure the payment of the same by mortgage or deed of trust on the whole or any part thereof of the said railroad, property, and income of the company then existing, or thereafter to be acquired; and may annex to said mortgage bonds the privilege of converting the same into the capital stock of the company, at par, at the option of the holders, if such election be signified in writing to the company three years before the maturity of said bonds.

May sell bonds. SEC. 13. That the directors of said company be and they are hereby authorized to negotiate and sell the bonds of the said company, at such times and in such places, either within or without this State, and at such rates and for such prices as, in their opinion, will best advance the interest of the company; and if such bonds are thus negotiated or sold at a discount below their par value, such sale shall be as valid and binding on the company, in every respect, as if they were sold or disposed of at their par value.

Trust deed and mortgage. SEC. 14. That the said company, in securing the payment of said bonds by a mortgage or deed of trust on the road, property, and income of the company, shall have power to execute a mortgage or deed of trust, aforesaid, to receive the payment of the full amount of bonds, which the company may at the time said mortgage or deed of trust bears date, or at any time thereafter, desire to sell or dispose of, and may execute and sell, from time to time, such amounts of said bonds, and of such dates, and payable to such persons, as the directors of said company may deem advisable, till the whole amount of bonds mentioned in such mortgage or deed of trust is executed and sold; and the said mortgage or deed of trust shall be as valid and effectual to secure the payment of the bonds so executed and sold, and every part thereof, as if the same, and every part thereof, had been executed with even date with the said mortgage or deed of trust.

SEC. 15. This act shall be deemed a public act, and is hereby so declared, and shall be favorably construed for all purposes herein expressed and declared, in all courts and places whatsoever, and shall be in force from and after its passage.

Approved February 16, 1865.

ORGANIZATION OF THE COMPANY.

In accordance with the provisions of the foregoing charter, books of subscription to the capital stock of the Atlantic and Pacific Railroad Company, were opened by Darwin Harvey, Azariah T. Galt and Elliott Anthony on the first day of June, A. D. 1870, and on the twenty-eighth day of June, A. D. 1870, the Atlantic and Pacific Railroad Company was duly organized according to law, and on the 6th day of February, 1872, at a regular meeting of the stockholders of said company, held at the office of the company in the city of Chicago, the following board of directors were elected: Roselle M. Hough, Thomas S. Dobbins, George Youngs, Walter L. Pease, John S. Wilcox, Harry Fox, and George S. Bowen.

The board at once proceeded to an organization by electing Roselle M. Hough, president; Thomas S. Dobbins, vice-president; Chauncey T. Bowen, treasurer; William T. Hughes, secretary; and John S. Wilcox, attorney.

CHANGE OF NAME.

At a regular meeting of the board of directors, held at their office on the twenty-sixth day of December, A. D. 1871, the following resolution was unanimously adopted:

"*Resolved*, That the name of the Atlantic and Pacific Railroad Company be changed to that of the Chicago and Pacific Railroad Company, and that the requisite steps be taken immediately by the board of directors to secure the same."

(This action was deemed necessary by the directors, there being another railroad of the same name in operation in the West.)

Under the provisions of an Act of the Legislature of the State of Illinois, entitled an act to provide for changing the names of incorporated companies, approved March twenty-sixth, 1872, and in accordance with the law in such cases made and provided, due notice thereof having been given to each stockholder by mail, and by publication in a newspaper as required by said act, a meeting of the stockholders of the Atlantic and Pacific Railroad Company was held at the general office of the company in the city of Chicago, and State of Illinois, on the thirtieth day of April, A. D. 1872, and at such meeting the following resolution was unanimously adopted by the affirmative vote of more than two-thirds of all the votes represented by the whole stock of said corporation.

"*Resolved*, That in accordance with the provisions of an act of the legislature of the State of Illinois, entitled an act to provide for changing the name of incorporated companies, approved March twenty-sixth, 1872, the name of the Atlantic and Pacific Railroad Company be changed to that of the Chicago and Pacific Railroad Company."

Which said change of name was published for three successive weeks in the Chicago *Evening Post*, as required by law.

[*Extract from an Ordinance of City Council of Chicago.*]

On the twelfth day of June, A. D. 1872, the common council of the city of Chicago passed an ordinance granting "permission and authority to the Chicago and Pacific Railroad Company and to its successors, to put down, construct, and maintain a railroad with a single or double track, and all necessary switches and turn-outs, along and upon the following named routes and streets in the city of Chicago: Commencing at the western limits of the city, at Bloomingdale road (or street), thence on said Bloomingdale road to and across Coventry street, thence on any property said company may acquire, by purchase, condemnation, or otherwise, to the North Branch of the Chicago river, thence across said North Branch and on any property said company may acquire by purchase, condemnation, or otherwise, to Jones avenue, thence on said Jones avenue and Hawthorne avenue to Willow street, thence on any property said company may acquire by purchase, condemnation, or otherwise, to North avenue; thence across North avenue to Cherry avenue; thence on Cherry avenue to and across the North branch canal; thence on Cherry avenue and North Branch street to and across the North Branch canal and to Hawthorne avenue; and from said North Branch street on any property said company may acquire by purchase, condemnation, or otherwise, west of Larrabee street and east of the North Branch of the Chicago river to Chicago avenue. And also to put down, construct, and maintain, for passenger cars only, a single or double track from the north side of said Willow street on said Hawthorne avenue to Larrabee street, with authority to run their cars over and along said tracks with steam or other power as said company may deem best."

RESOLUTION OF DIRECTORS ACCEPTING ORDINANCE.

At a regular meeting of the board of directors of the Chicago and Pacific Railroad, held at the office of the company, in the city of Chicago, on the 17th day of June, 1872, the following resolution was introduced, and adopted by the unanimous vote of said board; to-wit.:

Resolved, That the ordinance entitled "An Ordinance concerning the Chicago and Pacific Railroad Company, and the Chicago and Evanston Railroad Company," passed by the common council of the city of Chicago on the 12th day of June, 1872, and approved by Hon. Joseph Medill, mayor of said city, on the 14th day of June, A. D. 1872, be and the same is hereby accepted and approved, so far as the terms and provisions thereof pertain to said Chicago and Pacific Railroad Company.

SKETCH OF THE COUNTRY

THROUGH WHICH THE

CHICAGO AND PACIFIC RAILROAD PASSES.

The section of country through which the road passes is now the richest in the State of Illinois, and is destined to be one of the wealthiest and most populous portions of the American continent. Situated, as it is, directly upon the great highway of commerce between the Atlantic and Pacific coasts, over which must pass not only the immense traffic of the great producing Western States and rapidly improving Territories, to Chicago, as the grand receptacle for the agricultural products of the West, and the depot for the distribution of the manufactured articles of Illinois, Iowa, Wisconsin, Michigan, Missouri, Ohio, Indiana and the Middle and Eastern States, but also the international commerce of Europe and the East Indies, China and Japan.

It is but a few years since the first iron-working establishment was put in operation in Northern Illinois, and already it is predicted that the country comprised within a circle of one hundred miles around Chicago is to be the future iron center of America. Its direct communication by water with the great iron mines of the Lake Superior region affording the cheapest kind of transportation for the ore, and its close proximity to the endless fields of block coal of Indiana, which the most eminent scientists of the United States agree in pronouncing the best yet discovered for the manufacture of iron and steel, form the basis for this prediction. Whether it will ever be literally fulfilled or not, the future alone can tell; but it is certain that Northern Illinois, with its magnificent water power, and with iron ore and coal so easy of access, must inevitably do a very large amount of manufacturing.

FROM CHICAGO TO ELGIN.

Leaving the city of Chicago by Bloomingdale avenue, the road passes through the towns of Jefferson, Leyden, Addison, Bloomingdale, and Hanover, in Cook and DuPage counties, to the city of Elgin, in Kane county, midway between the Wisconsin and the Galena Divisions of the Chicago and Northwestern Railway, at an average distance of five and a half miles from the Galena Division on the south, and seven and a half miles from the Wisconsin Division on the north. These towns are thickly settled by an intelligent, industrious and thrifty population. The land is cut up into small farms, which are not only well improved, but fully stocked with everything which makes agriculture profitable; and nearly every acre of the ground is under a high state of cultivation. Large quantities of fruit and vegetables are raised, as well as small grains and stock. The milk, butter and cheese of this region are unsurpassed by any in the State; and for all their products a ready market is found in Chicago.

Heretofore, a large portion of the farmers of this rich tract of country, which is so intimately connected with Chicago, have been obliged to cart their produce from four to eight miles to a depot or haul to Chicago to get it to market.

They are fully alive to the importance of a line of railroad which will give them facilities for getting to and from their market, and liberal subscriptions to the capital stock of the company have been obtained from persons living along the line of the road between Chicago and Elgin. The right of way has also been obtained upon very reasonable terms.

MILK SHIPPED TO CHICAGO.

Some idea of the quantity of milk shipped to Chicago from the country between Chicago and the Fox river, through which the Chicago and Pacific Railroad passes, may be obtained by a perusal of the following figures, compiled from the official report of the proceedings of the Northwestern Dairyman's Association, held at Elgin, Illinois, January 16th, 17th and 18th, 1872.

NAME OF STATION.	No. of Gallons.	Amount of Freight Paid.
Dundee	859,544	$21,623 80
Elgin	86,990	2,174 85
Clintonville	39,028	980 40
Wayne	34,248	856 15
Elmhurst	91,000	1,820 00
Huntley	24,364	648 00
Turner Junction	23,470	588 00
Dunton	182,666	4,613 25
Barrington	122,551	905 55
Gilberts	361,452	14,415 00
Totals	1,825,313	$48,625 00

In addition to the milk shipped to Chicago, there is an immense quantity which is manufactured into butter and cheese; and it is estimated that the income to this road from milk and its products alone will amount to over one hundred thousand dollars in 1873.

SUBURBAN TOWNS.

Arrangements are already making for building several suburban towns along the line of the road between Chicago and Elgin by capitalists of Chicago, which will at once make a large business for the suburban trains which will be placed upon the road and run regularly by the first of March, 1873.

The first of the suburban towns is

HUMBOLDT,

Situated on the Boulevard leading from Humboldt park to Lincoln park, four miles and three-quarters from the Chicago Court-House, and a quarter of a mile north from Humboldt park. Mr. Henry Greenebaum, the German banker of Chicago, Charles Proebsting, Franz Arnold, and other capitalists, are largely interested in this beautiful suburb, and they have nearly completed a number of dwellings, which will be occupied by the first of January, and the town will be rapidly built up. An artesian well is being sunk, and a handsome depot, with tastefully arranged grounds, has been built. Mr. Greenebaum and the gentlemen interested with him in Humboldt, are determined to make it so pleasant and attractive as to induce a large migration to it from the city. It is expected that from seventy-five to one hundred houses will be erected at this station alone, during 1873, which will be occupied entirely by persons doing business in the city. At

ALMIRA,

Half a mile west of Humboldt, a town has been laid out, and improvements of a permanent nature will be commenced early in the spring. No expense will be spared to make this an attractive point, and a thriving village will soon be built.

The third suburban station is

PACIFIC,

Which is only six and a quarter miles from the Court-House in Chicago, and is located upon a beautiful tract of land, which has been laid out in large lots to accommodate the better class of people who are seeking homes out of the noise and dust of the city. Streets are being graded; an artesian well sunk; and sidewalks laid. Contracts have been made for the erection of a number of houses in the spring; and from the liberal spirit which has been manifested by the owners of the land in and about Pacific, in laying out and improving the town, it is certain that it will become a very popular suburb.

FORTY-SIXTH STREET CROSSING AND KELVYN GROVE.

At west Forty-Sixth street, half a mile beyond Pacific, and three-quarters of a mile west of the city limits, is the crossing of the new line of the Chicago & Northwestern Railway.

This crossing, with the station next west, will accommodate the large population soon to occupy the extensive and beautiful subdivision now being prepared for market, by the Hon. S. S. Hayes.

The entire tract embraces seven hundred and fifty acres, elevated from twenty-five to forty feet above Lake Michigan, partly fine oak groves, and is being laid out upon a scale of grandeur scarcely paralleled in the suburbs of any city.

The leading feature is a boulevard two hundred feet wide, upon which there are six miles of frontage in this property. There are, besides, eighteen miles of frontage on streets one hundred feet wide, and as much more upon streets sixty-six feet wide — on all of which a uniform building line is established from fifteen to thirty feet back from the front. The lots are large and deep.

Five thousand shade trees have been planted this spring, defining the blocks. The streets are to be graded and sidewalks made, and the erection of churches, school-houses, and a large number of dwelling-houses, is expected soon to be commenced.

GALEWOOD

Is the name of a station which has been located at a point two and a quarter miles from the city limits. The land here rises from sixty to eighty feet above the level of Lake Michigan, and is beautifully situated for a suburban town.

MONT CLARE,

The next station, is only a mile and a half from Corrinna, and is on high land which overlooks the surrounding country, offering superior locations for building sites.

ORISON,

A mile west of Sayer, is handsomely located for a suburban station, and will be laid out in large lots, which will attract the best class of residents who desire to leave the city for homes in the country.

At Galewood, Mont Clare and Orison, commodious and elegant depot buildings have been erected, and a fine business is springing up. Large quantities of building materials have already been contracted for, and are being taken out to these stations by the trains: and from present indications it is expected that one hundred houses will be erected at each of these stations during the year 1873.

The road crosses the Aux Plaines river at

RIVER PARK,

At a distance of only eight miles from the city limits of Chicago. Situated in the midst of a fine grove of timber, on a river affording natural facilities for drainage such as few towns possess, River Park will be one of the most beautiful and attractive suburban places within a radius of twenty miles from Chicago.

The company have determined to run hourly trains, equipped with all the modern improvements, from the city to River Park, stopping at every station, and carrying passengers at low rates of fare. They are assured of a large and paying business for their suburban trains at once, from the fact that hundreds of families are preparing to move on to the line of the road to avail themselves of the advantages offered by the company, as it is understood that one of the specialties of the Chicago & Pacific Railroad will be the accommodation of the suburban travel; and as no other road has ever made any especial effort in that direction, it is fair to suppose that with the inducements of cheap fares, hourly trains, superior accommodations, and healthy, thriving towns, the company will secure a large income from this source alone.

Between River Park and ELGIN, a distance of twenty-three miles, there will be several stations, from which a large business will be derived: especially will this be the case at

ROSELLE.

Twenty-four miles from Chicago, in the centre of four very rich townships is Roselle. It is the centre of the four very rich townships of Bloomingdale, Schaumberg, Elk Grove and Addison, which is destined to be at no distant day an important suburban town. The people of the four townships named above, who are all wealthy farmers, will make this their market town, and already lumber and coal yards are being opened here — a store, blacksmith and wagon shop, a mill, and other requisites for a town.

It is estimated that the business of Roselle will amount to thirty thousand dollars the first year, and will of course increase considerably every year with the increase of population and the natural growth of the country. Arrangements are making for sinking an artesian well, and a large tract (1,000 acres) of beautiful land is being laid out into large lots by one of the most eminent landscape gardeners in the West, which will prove very attractive to persons desirous of securing a desirable suburban home. This town is situated on a high and rolling prairie, interspersed with groves of native trees, which give it a very picturesque appearance.

The country immediately adjoining Roselle is well watered by springs and small streams, affording rich pasturage which will support a large number of the finest dairy farms in the State.

There are now within a few miles of Roselle eight cheese factories, the product of which will be shipped to Chicago over the Chicago & Pacific Railroad.

ELGIN,

AND ITS MANUFACTURES.

The road crosses the Fox river at Elgin, at a distance of thirty-five (35) miles from Chicago, being eight miles shorter than the line of the Galena Division of the Northwestern Railway, which also crosses the Fox river at this point.

Elgin is a city of seven thousand inhabitants, beautifully situated on both sides of the Fox river, which is one of the most picturesque and lovely streams in the State. On the west side of the river rises a high bluff which extends the whole length of the city, and is occupied by many handsome residences. On the east side, and near the river, is the principal business portion of the city, and the manufacturing establishments.

Surrounding the city, on every side, are hills and valleys which are unsurpassed for beauty and healthfulness by any other locality in the State, and which will in the course of a very few years be covered by the villas and elegant country residences of many of the capitalists and business men of Chicago.

The great Chicago fire of October 8th and 9th, 1871, which startled the world by the extent of the city burned over, the tremendous loss, and the suddenness with which one hundred thousand persons were rendered homeless, led thousands of business men, who had resided in the city for years, to seek a home for their families where they would be free from the liability of ever again witnessing a repetition of the fearful scenes of that terrible conflagration.

In selecting a home out of the city, the first things thought of are, a healthy location, pleasant scenery, and satisfactory church and school accommodations. In all of these respects Elgin is unsurpassed by any city of its size in Illinois. It is one of the most healthful localities in the State, and, so far as scenery is concerned, it is all that could be desired. With its beautiful river running through the center of the city, its hills and groves on every side, making the choicest building sites that can be found anywhere, and a gravel subsoil which precludes the idea of mud, it presents a combination of attractions such as very few places in the West, and *none* within the same distance from Chicago, possess. Add to these its excellent public schools, which are a credit to the city—the Elgin Academy, a superior institution, conducted upon liberal and unsectarian principles, and accommodating some four hundred students—its thirteen churches, representing all denominations—an opera-house seating fifteen hundred persons—the city lighted by gas—a well-organized fire department—and an intelligent, industrious, law-abiding population, and you will see at once that Elgin is destined to be one of the most popular suburban cities in Northern Illinois.

The Fox river affords a splendid water power, and the close proximity of Elgin to Chicago, and also to the great coal fields of Illinois and Indiana, make it one of the most desirable locations for manufacturing establishments in the West. It is already becoming widely known as a manufacturing center; and with the impetus which will be given to it by the completion of the Chicago and Pacific Railroad, it must of necessity become one of the principal manufacturing towns of Illinois.

Among the important manufacturing establishments now in full operation in the city are the works of

THE NATIONAL (ELGIN) WATCH COMPANY,

Which began operations in 1867, and now own property in buildings, machinery, etc., to the value of over *one million dollars*. They have in their employ over *six hundred* persons, who turn out nearly *two hundred* perfect watches every day.

The monthly pay-roll of the company now amounts to over *thirty thousand dollars*.

The employees of this great establishment are well educated, refined, intelligent and enterprising citizens; many of whom own handsome homes here, and are foremost in all works for the improvement of the city. Several of the men employed by the National Watch Company are among the most eminent skilled mechanics in the United States, and the manufacture of watches is the most delicate mechanical work known, requiring a scientific knowledge vastly superior to the majority of mechanical employments.

In 1867 the company turned out *three thousand* watches; in 1869 the product was over *twenty-two thousand*; and for the year 1872 they will probably make over *fifty thousand*; and even then they will be unable to fill the orders which they now have on hand.

The success of this company is unprecedented in the history of the world; their watches are to be found in every part of the globe which has been visited by civilized man; and they are still improving their production and extending their business.

The location of their works at Elgin has been of immense importance to the city; and the company have done more than all else to bring Elgin before the world as a manufacturing center. Their business is increasing so rapidly that the frequent enlargement of their works is necessitated; and it is expected that within a few years the company will employ from fifteen hundred to two thousand operatives.

THE FOX RIVER MANUFACTURING COMPANY

Have a first-class woolen mill, in which they give employment to a large number of men. They are manufacturing cassimeres, flannels, and other goods of a high grade, and their business is rapidly increasing.

THE ELGIN MILK-CONDENSING COMPANY

Is one of the largest establishments of the kind in the country, and the product of their Elgin works is used in almost every country on the globe. Gail Borden, of New York, is the president of the company, and to his untiring energy and zeal is largely due the great success of the enterprise. The company does a very large business, and in 1871 paid the Northwestern Railway over $6,000.00 for freight alone.

THE ELGIN IRON-WORKS

Is an important establishment of the kind, and is doing a large business, which has been nearly doubled in the past two years. The fact that the iron ore of Lake Superior can be landed on the

Chicago and Pacific Railroad Company's docks in Chicago, and shipped to Elgin at less expense than it would require to cart it to the remote parts of Chicago, and the further fact that the celebrated block coal of Indiana (which is unsurpassed by any coal in the world for iron-working) can be shipped to Elgin by the Chicago and Pacific Railroad without reloading, and at very slight expense, makes it almost certain that Elgin will, within a few years, become largely interested in the manufacture of iron. A proposition is already on foot to establish iron-works there which will employ several hundred workmen.

THE ELGIN DAIRY COMPANY,

Established in 1870, is doing a large business in the manufacture of butter and cheese, and has already established a reputation for its products which is second to none in the country. By the market reports it will be seen that the Elgin Dairy Co.'s. cheese and butter command a higher price than any other brands in the market.

THE ELGIN PACKING COMPANY,

Have extensive works on the west side of the river for packing or hermetically sealing tomatoes, corn, and every variety of fruit. A large and profitable business is being done, and it is increasing constantly.

THE PHŒNIX FOUNDRY

Is quite a large establishment, devoted principally to the manufacture of school furniture and other light castings, which are all shipped to Chicago. The facilities of this establishment will be greatly increased within a year, and the business nearly doubled.

OTHER ESTABLISHMENTS.

Among the manufacturing establishments of less importance, but which are doing a considerable business in their various lines, may be named five wagon and carriage shops, a plow factory, a washing-machine and packing-box factory, a reaper factory, a large brick yard, two planing mills, a sash, door and blind factory, a shoe factory, and four flouring mills.

In addition to the above manufacturing establishments, there are two first-class newspaper and printing offices, two national banks, and over sixty mercantile houses.

There is also a large amount of wool, grain and pork purchased here, nearly all of which is shipped to Chicago.

The receipts of the Chicago and Northwestern Railway from the business of Elgin during the year 1871, were as follows:

From freight	$71,681.89
From passengers	61,923.60
Total Receipts	$133,605.49

From the foregoing statistics, it will be seen that the already large business of Elgin must increase with every succeeding year, and the Chicago and Pacific Railroad Company confidently expect, that, having shortened the distance between Chicago and Elgin over eight miles, by building an air-line road, and by this means given greatly increased facilities to manufacturers and all other branches of business, that their receipts from the business of Elgin within three years from date, will exceed one hundred thousand dollars per annum.

FROM ELGIN TO BYRON.

From the Fox river west, the road passes through the towns of Elgin, Plato, Burlington and Hampshire in Kane county; Genoa, Kingston and Franklin in De Kalb county; and Monroe, Scott and Marion in Ogle county, to Byron on the Rock river, eighty-four miles west of Chicago, all of which are old and thickly-settled towns, and which will give the road a large business in both passengers and freight.

Between Elgin and Byron (a distance of fifty miles) the line is distant twelve miles from the Galena Division of the Northwestern Railroad on the north, and fourteen miles from the Iowa Division of the Northwestern on the south.

This section of country is at present largely devoted to stock raising, which is a very profitable business here. When the stock is ready for market it is shipped to Chicago, and heretofore many of the farmers have been obliged to drive their stock from twelve to eighteen miles to a depot.

Appreciating the advantages which will accrue to them from the completion of a road through their country, the people living along the line of the road from Elgin to Byron have subscribed liberally to the capital stock of the company. In addition to this, they will aid by every means in their power the speedy completion of the road.

BYRON.

ITS WATER-POWER AND NATURAL ADVANTAGES.

The village of Byron is situated on the west bank of the Rock river, at a distance of eighty-four miles from Chicago.

The Rock river at this point is over seven hundred feet wide, and will furnish the grandest water-power in the State of Illinois. Its bed is solid rock, and on either side of it are inexhaustible quarries of stone, suitable for building purposes, which will be a source of revenue to the road as soon as the track reaches them.

A more beautiful location cannot be found in the West. Situated, as it is, on a high and level plateau, surrounded by a country which is unsurpassed in beauty and fertility, and with the Rock river running through it, between magnificent bluffs which remind one of the beautiful scenery of the Upper Mississippi, it is truly a most delightful place for a town.

The want of railroad facilities has greatly retarded the prosperity and growth of the village, the larger proportion of the trade of the country being done at the place of marketing the produce of the farmers, which is at present principally at Rockford, fifteen miles up the river.

Notwithstanding the fact that the farmers have heretofore been compelled to transport their produce to market with teams a distance of ten to twenty miles, thrift and enterprise are seen on all sides, and the buildings and other improvements will compare favorably with any other section of the State.

It is for the same reason that one of the best and most extensive water-powers to be found in the State lies unimproved.

By the completion of the Chicago and Pacific Railroad, Byron will be brought nearer to Chicago than any other town on the Rock river, and with the facilities which the road will give to it, it will, without doubt, become within a few years an important manufacturing center.

FROM BYRON TO THE MISSISSIPPI.

West of the village of Byron the road passes through the towns of Byron, Leaf River, Maryland and Forreston, in Ogle county, and thence through the northern part of Carroll and southern portions of Stephenson and Jo Daviess counties, to a point on the Mississippi river opposite Bellevue, Iowa.

This entire district of country, from Byron to the Mississippi, which is rich, productive, and under a high state of cultivation, and is at present without any direct railroad connection with Chicago, will give the road a large local business at once.

The completion of the road to Bellevue will necessitate the erection of a grain elevator at that point to accommodate the immense grain trade of Eastern Iowa and the Upper Mississippi which will reach the Chicago market by this route.

BELLEVUE, IOWA,

Is a rapidly-growing town of about two thousand inhabitants, situated on the west bank of the Mississippi river, about twenty miles south of Dubuque. It is the market town of Jackson county, and will doubtless become a very important point. The people of Bellevue and vicinity are anxious to have the road built, and will give the company material aid to secure its speedy completion.

TRIBUTARY OR BRANCH ROADS,

AND

Western and Northern Connections.

THE SYCAMORE BRANCH.

At Genoa (twenty miles west of Elgin) the road will be connected with Sycamore (the county seat of De Kalb county) by a branch road eight miles in length, which will be built by the citizens of Sycamore and of the country adjacent to it, and operated by this company, the completion of this branch will give to the Chicago and Pacific Railroad a large portion of the business of the city of Sycamore and the rich country tributary to it. Sycamore has a population of over three thousand. It contains several manufacturing establishments, including the celebrated "Marsh Harvester," besides a number of cheese factories, etc.; several churches and fine graded schools. There is also a grain elevator here, the proprietors of which buy large quantities of grain, making this the principal grain market of this section. Nearly all the grain and other products are shipped to Chicago.

THE BELVIDERE BRANCH.

The people of Belvidere and the residents of the section of country lying between Belvidere and Genoa, will probably build a branch road from Belvidere to Genoa to connect with the Chicago and Pacific Railroad, which will give to this company not only a large business from Belvidere and vicinity, but also the whole of the business for some miles each side of the branch road from Belvidere to Genoa. The city of Belvidere is the county seat of Boone county, and has a population of over four thousand inhabitants. It is situated on the Kishwaukee river, at a distance of seventy-eight miles from Chicago; and is the principal market town of the county.

JUNCTION WITH THE CHICAGO AND SUPERIOR RAILROAD.

Near the center of the beautiful Stillman Valley, eighty miles west of Chicago, about twelve and a half miles south of Rockford, the road will form a junction with the Chicago and Superior Railroad. This road will extend north through Rockford in Illinois, to Beloit, Janesville, or some point north of it, in Wisconsin, which will connect it with the great lumber regions of that State.

By this important connection the Chicago and Pacific will secure a share of the business of Rockford, one of the largest cities of Northern Illinois, and which contains at present more manufacturing establishments in successful operation than any other city in the State except Chicago. To the people of Rockford and vicinity, the completion of the Chicago and Pacific Railroad is looked forward to as an important event in their business history, as it will give a western and southern outlet for their manufactured articles, of which they have long felt a great want.

It will also give them a competing line to Chicago, which will be several miles shorter than the only road they now have. The connection of the Chicago and Pacific with the Chicago, Danville and Vincennes Railroad, by which the block and other coals of Indiana which are brought to Chicago by that road, can be shipped to any point on the Chicago and Pacific without reloading, is considered a very important one by manufacturers, and will be of great advantage to Elgin, Rockford, and other manufacturing cities.

ROCKFORD (THE FOREST CITY),

Situated on both sides of the Rock river, midway between Chicago and Galena, is one of the most beautiful and attractive places in the State. It has a population of fourteen thousand inhabitants, and with its magnificent water-power it has developed an immense manufacturing interest, which would very soon be doubled with the facilities which a competing road would give.

The following, compiled from statistics published in the Rockford *Journal* of March 16th, 1872, will give the reader some idea of the importance of Rockford as a manufacturing city:

MANUFACTURING INTERESTS OF ROCKFORD.

"One of the most important interests to the growth and prosperity of any community is that of manufactures.

We have taken pains to visit the various manufacturing establishments, and we feel that even our own citizens will be astonished at the magnitude of this interest. We condense, so far as possible, and present the following list·

One establishment will manufacture this season 1,000 cultivators.

Another, 1,300 corn cultivators, 300 broadcast seeders and cultivators, 100 to 200 Barnes self-rake, 200 Acme and 50 other mowers, 50 droppers and gleaners, 1,500 to 2,000 corn-planters, 200 double shovels, 1,000 to 2,000 caster colters; they also make iron furniture, school-seat castings, etc.

Another, 2,000 to 2,500 cultivators, 1,000 to 1,500 plows, 300 to 500 caster colters, besides a large number of harrows, planters, reapers and mowers, on which no approximation can be made.

Another, 500 to 700 plows, 300 to 400 caster colters.

Another, 1,500 to 2.000 cultivators, 300 to 500 reapers.

A cotton mill does a business to the value of $2,000 per week, in the manufacture principally of seamless bags.

Another establishment will manufacture 1.500 to 2,000 seeders, 300 to 500 corn-cultivators, 75 to 100 reapers.

Another, 900 to 1,000 seeders, 200 to 300 feed steamers.

Another, 800 to 1,200 cultivators, 300 to 500 gang plows, 400 to 600 sulky plows, 2,000 to 2,500 breaking plows, 6,000 to 8,000 stirring plows, 3,000 to 5,000 rolling colters.

Another, from 600 to 700 cultivators.

One paper mill, print and wrapping-paper manufacturers, consume about 1,500 tons of straw, and 1,400 tons of coal per annum, resulting in about 900 tons of paper.

The malleable iron works furnish extensive quantities of iron for reapers, cultivators, plows, etc. Plow clevises alone amount to 100,000. They use about 500 tons of pig iron, and 500 tons of hard coal.

Another manufacturer of iron, force, suction and lift pumps, and general jobbing, will make this season 3,000 pumps.

One firm of woolen manufacturers — 6,000 yards of cassimeres, 6,000 yards of flannels, 7,000 yards of repellants, 3 tons of wool into stocking yarn.

A carriage, plow and machine bolt factory turns out 10,000 per day.

Another firm manufacturing carpet warps and twines, do a business to the value of about $3,000 per week.

Another firm will manufacture 50,000 butter tubs.

Another, about 30,000 flour barrels and tubs.

The clothes-pin factory is turning off from 250 to 300 gross per day.

The wire works — 250,000 to 300,000 feet of wire cloth, 10,000 dozen sieves, 25,000 dozen riddles, coal sifters, screens, etc.

One firm manufacture carriage, machine bolts, sickles, etc. Of bolts, they turn off 4,000 per day, and will manufacture this season 1,000 sickles.

Door, Sash and Blinds.—This interest is of great importance, and gives employment to many men, but it is impossible to approximate the number of articles manufactured.

The Rockford Wind Mill. Will make this season from 800 to 1,000.

Wooden Pumps.—This interest is also one of growing importance. There will be manufactured this season from 2,000 to 3,000.

There are five flouring mills, with a capacity of 1,800 barrels per day.

The manufacturers of first-class carriages will build this season from 400 to 450. They find it difficult to fill orders with their present facilities, and will soon enlarge.

Hands Employed.— In the above list of our leading manufacturers, are employed nearly 1,200 hands, the large majority of whom are heads of families. Taking the usual standard, that a family will average four persons, it is not an unreasonable statement to make, that our manufacturers are feeding at least 4,000 mouths — nearly one-third of our entire population.

If, then, manufacturing is of such vast importance to our community, how anxious should our capitalists and people be to augment and encourage this great interest! Let us welcome every enterprising firm or man — extend the warmest hand — and with the near approach of additional railroad facilities, who can tell what Rockford may yet be?"

JUNCTION WITH THE ILLINOIS CENTRAL RAILROAD.

At Forreston, in Ogle county, nine miles south of Freeport, the road crosses the main line of the Illinois Central Railroad, at a distance of a little less than one hundred miles from Chicago. By making a connection at this point with the Chicago and Pacific, the Illinois Central will have the shortest line from Dubuque to Chicago upon which to run their trains; and an arrangement of this kind will undoubtedly be made between the two companies, as the Illinois Central owns no line from the west to Chicago.

This will give to the Chicago and Pacific a very large business, as the traffic between Chicago and Dubuque (the key city of Iowa) is of itself sufficient to pay for the operating of a line of railroad between the two cities.

The Illinois Central Company, in addition to their Illinois lines, are now operating, under a long lease, the Dubuque and Sioux City Railroad, which extends across the State of Iowa from Dubuque, on the Mississippi river, to Sioux City on the Missouri river They are also operating a line of road of about one hundred and thirty miles in length, extending from Cedar City, on the Dubuque and Sioux City Railroad, to Austin, Minnesota.

These two roads give to the Illinois Central an immense business, a large portion of which goes to Chicago; and upon the completion of the Chicago and Pacific Railroad all of their Chicago business will undoubtedly go over this road, as such an arrangement will save them over twenty miles in distance, and more than an hour in time.

THE WARREN AND MINERAL POINT BRANCH.

The people of Warren, with the capitalists of Mineral Point and others who are interested in the mines of that section, are making arrangements to construct a branch road, some twenty miles in length, from Berriman, in Jo Daviess county, at a distance of thirty-five miles west from Byron, to Warren, in Jo Daviess county, to connect at the latter place with the Platteville and Mineral Point Railroad, which taps the rich mineral country north of Galena. From this section a large business may be expected. The people living along the line are anxious to have this branch built, which will give them direct communication with Chicago, and thus increase the value of their products.

CONNECTION WITH THE DUBUQUE AND MINNESOTA R. R.

At Bellevue, Iowa, the road will connect with the Dubuque and Minnesota Railroad, which extends from Clinton to St. Paul, and which will doubtless give the C. & P. a large business in both passengers and freight, as it will furnish them almost an air line across the State of Illinois from the Mississippi river to Chicago.

GRAVEL FOR BALLAST.

For miles each side of the Fox River, there are inexhaustable beds of the finest gravel immediately adjoining the track, and so situated as to be easily worked at all seasons of the year, which will be of immense value to the Company in furnishing ballast for the road bed. There is also plenty of gravel at Byron, on the Rock river, and at several other points between Elgin and the Mississippi, where all the ballast which will ever be required for the entire road can be easily and cheaply obtained.

TABLE "A.,"

Compiled from the official record of the proceedings of the Illinois State Board of Equalization, and showing the valuation of real and personal property in the counties of Illinois traversed by and contiguous to the Chicago and Pacific Railroad, on the first day of April, A. D. 1872:

COUNTIES.	Personal Property.	Railroad Property.	Lands.	Town and City Lots.	Total Property
DuPage	$2,594,875	$1,795,330	$10,609,690	$ 1,438,960	$16,438,855
Kane..	8,195,290	2,990,685	17,691,130	12,239,100	41,116,205
De Kalb....	3,807,628	727,628	12,058,644	1,521,748	18,115,648
Ogle........	5,737,173	485,040	11,935,287	1,697,097	19,854,597
Boone	1,775,175	672,006	3,977,472	721,248	7,145,901
Winnebago .	4,389,396	1,211,082	8,332,287	4,205,907	18,138,672
Stephenson .	3,534,090	486,132	9,598,557	1,959,453	15,578,232
Carroll	2,223,180	450,951	5,230,233	770,247	8,674,611
Jo Daviess..	3,327,567	480,000	4,620,036	1,327,941	9,755,544
Totals....	$35,584,374	$9,298,854	$84,053,336	$25,881,701	$154,818,265

TABLE "B,"

Showing the population in 1860 and 1871, of the counties of Illinois traversed by and contiguous to the road, and the increase in population during the last eleven years:

Name of County.	Population in 1860.	Population in 1871.	Increase in 11 years.
DuPage	14,696	17,285	2,589
Kane	30,024	41,791	11,767
De Kalb	19,079	24,175	5,096
Boone	11,670	13,542	1,872
Ogle	22,863	29,293	6,430
Winnebago	24,457	30,801	6,344
Carroll	11,718	18,205	6,487
Stephenson	25,112	32,218	7,106
Jo Daviess	27,147	27,800	653
Totals	186,766	235,110	48,344

By reference to the above table, it will be seen that the population of the counties traversed by and contiguous to the Chicago and Pacific Railroad has increased very considerably during the past eleven years; and the rapid development of manufactures through this section of the State must inevitably largely increase the population each year, giving to this company a lucrative business from the start, and which will continue to increase with succeeding years.

TABLE "C."

In the foregoing tables of the value of real and personal property, the increase in population, etc., in the counties of Illinois traversed by and contiguous to the Chicago and Pacific, the county of Cook, in which is the eastern terminus of the road, and through which it runs for a distance of over twenty miles, has been omitted, and is here given by itself:

The population of Cook county in 1860 was 143,947; in 1871 it was 403,750—showing an increase in eleven years of over 259,000 persons.

The following figures, compiled from the official record of the proceedings of the Illinois State Board of Equalization, show the valuation of real and personal property in the county of Cook, on the first day of April, A. D. 1872:

Personal Property.	Railroad Property.	Lands.	Town and City Lots.	Total Property.
$53,865,186	$9,171,741	$32,213,184	$186,278,286	$281,528,397

The figures given in the foregoing tables are far below the real value of the property mentioned, as it is estimated that from one-fourth to one-third of the entire property in this State escapes taxation; and also that property, as a rule, is assessed at much less than its real value. So that to show the actual value, from twenty-five to forty per cent. should be added to the amounts here given.

LOCAL BUSINESS.

EXTRACT FROM THE RAILROAD COMMISSIONER'S REPORT.

The State Board of Railroad and Warehouse Commissioners of Illinois, in their first annual report to the Governor, issued January, 1872—after giving in detail the statistics of the business of the various railroad companies doing business in Illinois—say that THE LOCAL TRAFFIC IS MUCH THE LARGEST PORTION OF THE BUSINESS OF ALL RAILROADS, BEING IN THIS STATE RARELY IF EVER LESS THAN NINETY PER CENT. OF THE GROSS EARNINGS.

THE CHICAGO AND ALTON RAILROAD

In the Ninth Annual Report of the President and Directors of the Chicago and Alton Railroad Company for the year ending December 31st, 1871, issued February, 1872, they make the following statement:

PASSENGERS.

"This Company transported during the year 1871, seven hundred and fifteen thousand six hundred and sixty-two (715,662) passengers, and of the entire passenger traffic for the year, *ninety-four and six-tenths per cent.* traveled between local stations, and five and four-tenths per cent. were through passengers."

Nearly ninety-five per cent. of the passenger traffic being local business.

FREIGHT.

In the same report they say:

"The proportion between through and local freights being 10.46 per cent. of the former to 89.54 per cent. of the latter."

Nearly ninety per cent. of the entire freight traffic of the road being local business.

The reports of a majority of the railroads of Illinois show that the local business is the principal source of their income, and that those roads which have a rich and prosperous section of country to back them—such as the Chicago and Pacific passes through—invariably pay.

CROSSING OF THE WESTERN UNION RAILROAD.

At Shannon, eight miles west of Forreston (see page 32) and twenty miles east of Savanna, the Chicago & Pacific crosses the Western Union Railroad, at a distance of one hundred and thirteen and a half miles from Chicago via the Chicago & Pacific, and one hundred and seventy-nine miles from Chicago via the Western Union.

In the official report of the business of the Western Union Railroad for 1872, the following statistics are given:

"Abstract of freight forwarded from Shannon, Lanark, Mt. Carroll, Savanna and Thompson stations, by the Western Union Railroad during the year 1872:

Wheat, Rye, Barley, Oats, etc.	2,032,524	bushels.
Flour	3,775	barrels.
Pork and Beef	1,378	"
Dressed Hogs	692,660	lbs.
Eggs	210,700	"
Butter	145,170	"
Lard and Tallow	399,320	"
Wool	4,730	"
Hides	54,230	"
Merchandise	279,370	"
Machinery	22,200	"
Agricultural Implements	546,770	"
Horses and Horned Cattle	3,098	No.
Hogs and Sheep	34,072	"
Lumber	146,000	feet.
Brick	58,300	No.
Miscellaneous	4,094,380	lbs."

From the fact that a large proportion of this traffic naturally belongs to Chicago — as the great grain and produce market of the world — and would go there if it could be reached by a direct line, it is certain that eventually it will go via the Chicago & Pacific Railroad.

TO THE PRESIDENT AND BOARD OF DIRECTORS OF THE CHICAGO AND PACIFIC RAILROAD.

GENTLEMEN: I submit herewith to your Board, as requested, a statement of work done before and since the date of my taking charge (March 1st, 1873) of the line of the Chicago and Pacific Railroad, together with estimated cost of construction and completion of the road, by divisions.

FIRST DIVISION.

I found, on March 1st, the grading partially finished for 34 miles, or nearly to Fox river; 13 miles of iron laid from Chicago west, and sufficient cross-ties and material to complete the work to Elgin.

The alignment on the first division I find generally direct, the distance between Chicago and Elgin being 35 miles; while on the Chicago and Northwestern it is 42 miles.

The average grade per mile is 16.5 feet: the maximum grade 1 foot per 100, or 53 feet to the mile, for short distances.

As soon, after assuming charge, as the weather permitted, a force was put on the work sufficient to keep in advance of the track-laying, and by the 1st of June we expect to reach the city of Elgin.

The course of the road is through a well settled and rich section of country, for the most part consisting of undulating prairie and timber land, the details of which are correctly given in your published description.

ESTIMATED COST OF FIRST DIVISION C. & P. R. R.—CHICAGO TO ELGIN—DISTANCE 35 MILES.

Grading	$63,000 00	
Grubbing and clearing	600 00	
Right of way (including Chicago)	280,000 00	
		$343,600 00

SUPERSTRUCTURE.

Swing bridges	$27,491 00	
Trestle work	26,176 00	
Cattle passes, box culverts, cattle guards	7,000 00	
Track laying	14,000 00	
Cross ties	41,580 00	
Iron	283,500 00	
Fish plates, spikes and fastenings	32,770 00	
Crossings, frogs and switches	4,000 00	
Ballasting	28,000 00	
		$464,517 00
Water tanks and coal sheds	5,000 00	
Station houses	24,000 00	
Chicago buildings, engine house, repair shops and freight house	93,400 00	
		122,400 00
Motive power	68,420 00	
Rolling stock	114,960 00	
Fencing	21,700 00	
Engineering and stationery	7,000 00	
		212,080 00
Total		$1,142,597 00
Average per mile		$32,645 00

ESTIMATED RECEIPTS FROM THE FIRST DIVISION OF THE C. & P. R. R. — WHICH, WHEN COMPLETED, WILL EXTEND FROM CHICAGO TO ELGIN — DISTANCE, 35 MILES.

IN BOUND TRAFFIC.

U. S. mail per year	$ 1,560 00	
Express merchandise	3,120 00	
Milk, 5,660 tons	24,960 00	
Freight, 14,000 tons hauled, average distance 24 miles, regular rates	46,800 00	
Freight, 28,080 tons, special rates	37,440 00	
2,000 cars gravel and sand	18,720 00	
6,240 passengers, average distance 25 miles, regular rates	6,240 00	
18,720 passengers, average distance 25 miles, special rates	9,360 00	
		$148,200 00

OUT BOUND TRAFFIC.

U.S. mail per year	$1,560 00	
Express merchandise, per year	2,496 00	
14,000 tons freight hauled, average distance 24 miles, regular rates	46,800 00	
28,080 tons freight hauled, average distance 24 miles, special rates	37,440 00	
6,240 passengers, average distance 25 miles	6,240 00	
18,720 passengers, average distance 25 miles, special rates	9,360 00	
		$103,896 00
In bound traffic		148,200 00
Total		$252,096 00
60 per cent. for operating expenses		151,257 60
Net earnings per year		$100,838 40

Equal to 8 per cent. on $1,260,000 00.

The progress of these counties may be seen by the following statistics:

KANE COUNTY.

First settlement made in 1834.

The population in 1850 was	16,703
" " 1870 "	39,151
" " 1871 "	41,791
The census of 1870 gives value of real estate	$25,152,198
Value of personal property	8,030,019
" farm products one year	2,569,719

The report of the State board of equalization for April, 1872, gives:

Real estate	$29,930,230
Personal property	8,195,290
Railroad property	2,990,685

The valuation of real and personal property, from official record of October, 1871, in DeKalb and Ogle counties, gives:

Counties.	Horses, Cattle, Sheep, Hogs.	Railroad property.	Improved lands.	Unimproved lands.	Lands.	City and village lots.	All Real Estate.
DeKalb....	794,940	172,686	2,283,274	152,017	2,975,291	369,558	3,344,849
Ogle......	631,840	100.306	3,542,724	509.729	4.052.453	601,685	4.654,138

Total valuation of all property:

	DEKALB.	OGLE.
By town assessors.................	$4,518,632	$4,563,818
By State board....................	5,956,387	6,191,935

SECOND DIVISION.

FROM ELGIN TO BYRON.

From Elgin west our line passes through Kane, DeKalb and Ogle counties to Byron on the Rock river—distance from Chicago 85 miles, and from Elgin 50 miles. The alignment is direct, Byron being 7 miles north of Elgin; grade, average 22 feet to the mile, no grades exceeding our maximum grade of 53 to the mile.

At Byron the river bed is of rock, and large quantities of good building and dimension stone are adjacent and convenient to our line, from which we can supply the whole country bordering on our line with good building material. Hence the need of a railroad, especially an East and West line, has long been realized. The land in these counties is cultivated by the best class of farmers. The soil is of a deep black loam, and is widely known as a rich grazing, stock-raising and grain-producing region, watered by streams affording ample water-power for the grist and saw mills already in operation.

The Rock river runs north and south, centrally through Ogle county; the county is evenly divided between high rolling prairie and timber belts, which furnish fuel and building material.

ESTIMATED COST OF SECOND DIVISION OF THE C. & P. R. R.—FROM ELGIN TO BYRON—DISTANCE, 50 MILES.

Grading	$84,242 00	
Grubbing and clearing	1,000 00	
Right of way	60,000 00	
		$145,242 00
SUPERSTRUCTURE.		
Bridging, Howe truss and masonry	$60,000 00	
Trestle bridging	20,000 00	
Cattle passes, box culverts, cattle guards	5,000 00	
Cross ties	59,400 00	
Steel rails, 56 lbs	585,000 00	
Fish plates, fastenings and spikes	46,800 00	
Crossings, frogs and switches	3,000 00	
Ballasting	40,000 00	
		839,400 00
Engine houses and machine shops	133,450 00	
Station houses	15,000 00	
Water tanks and coal sheds	5,000 00	
		153,450 00
Fencing	31,000 00	
Motive power	97,744 00	
Rolling stock	164,230 00	
Engineering and stationery	14,524 00	
		307,498 00
Total		$1,445,590 00
Average per mile		$28,912 00

THIRD DIVISION,

EXTENDING FROM BYRON TO THE MISSISSIPPI RIVER—DISTANCE 48½ MILES.

From Byron our road passes through the following towns: Byron, Leaf River, Maryland and Forreston, in Ogle county; thence through the township of Shannon to Shannon in Carroll county, where we intersect with the Western Union Railroad—distance from Chicago, one hundred and thirteen and a half miles.

The intersecting north and south lines projected and under construction, whose outlet eastward will naturally be by the Chicago and Pacific railroad, will bring a large and remunerative business, and all await the completion of the Chicago and Pacific railroad with interest, as affording them a most important connection.

THIRD DIVISION CHICAGO & PACIFIC R. R.—BYRON TO THE MISSISSIPPI RIVER—48½ MILES. ESTIMATED COST TO SHANNON, WHERE WE CONNECT WITH THE WESTERN UNION R. R.—DISTANCE, 28 MILES FROM BYRON.

Grading	$52,935 00	
Grubbing and clearing	1,200 00	
Right of way	34,200 00	
		$88,335 00

SUPERSTRUCTURE.

Bridging and trestle work	$22,000 00	
Cattle passes, box culverts and cattle guards	3,000 00	
Track laying	11,400 00	
Cross ties	37,620 00	
Steel rail, 56 lbs. per yard	333,450 00	
Fish plates, fastenings and spikes	26,676 00	
Crossings, frogs and switches	2,500 00	
Ballasting	22,800 00	
		459,446 00

WATER TANKS, COAL SHEDS AND DEPOTS.

Water tanks and coal sheds	$3,000 00	
Station houses	6,000 00	
Engine houses and repair shops	128,150 00	
		137,150 00
Fencing	17,670 00	
Motive power	92,836 00	
Rolling stock	155,161 00	
Engineering and stationery	8,833 00	
		274,500 00
Total		$959,431 00
Average per mile		$33,664 00

SUMMARY.

ESTIMATED COST OF ROAD FROM CHICAGO TO SHANNON—DISTANCE, 113½ MILES.

Grading	$200,177 00	
Grubbing and clearing	2,800 00	
Right of way (including Chicago)	374,200 00	
		$577,177 00
SUPERSTRUCTURE.		
Truss bridging and masonry	$87,491 00	
Trestle work	68,176 00	
Cattle passes, box culverts, cattle guards	15,000 00	
Track laying	45,400 00	
Cross ties	138,600 00	
Iron, 56 lb rail on 1st division, steel rail on 2d and 3d divisions	1,201,950 00	
Fish plates, fastenings and spikes	106,246 00	
Crossings, frogs and switches	9,500 00	
Ballasting	90,800 00	
		1,763,163 00
WATER TANKS, COAL SHEDS AND DEPOTS.		
Water tanks and coal sheds	$13,000 00	
Station houses	45,000 00	
Engine houses and repair shops	355,000 00	
		413,000 00
Fencing	70,370 00	
Motive power	259,000 00	
Rolling stock	434,350 00	
Engineering and stationery	30,357 00	
		794,077 00
Total		$3,547,417 00
Average per mile		$31,255 00

The above estimate assumes the construction of a first class road in every respect; the road-bed, structures, &c., such as may be found on our best roads: the track provided with the most improved fastenings and completely ballasted.

It is the intention of the company to replace the iron on the first division with steel, at a cost of $150,000; and on the second and third divisions steel rail will be used throughout.

STATEMENT OF POPULATION BY COUNTIES, 1870.

On Main Line of Chicago & North-Western Railway, Iowa Division, Chicago to the Mississippi River, 138 miles.			On Galena Division Chicago & North-Western Railway, Chicago to the Mississippi River, 188 miles.			On Chicago & Pacific Railroad to the Mississippi River. Distance, 133 miles.		
Cook County	350,236		Cook County	350,236		Cook County	350,236	
Du Page "	16,761		Du Page "	16,761		Du Page "	16,761	
Kane "	38,974	38,974	Kane "	38,974	38,974	Kane "	38,974	38,974
De Kalb "	23,275	23,275	McHenry "	23,812	23,812	De Kalb "	23,275	23,275
Lee "	27,252	27,252	Boone "	13,007	13,007	Ogle "	27,539	27,539
Whiteside	27,512	27,512	Winnebago	29,373	29,373	Carroll "	16,707	16,707
			Stephenson	30,678	30,678			
			Jo Daviess	27,789	27,789			
Total	484,010	117,013		530,630	163,633		473,492	106,495
Average per mile	3,507	1,146		2,822	1,069		3,560	1,087

EARNINGS.

In place of submitting an estimate of the traffic to be secured from all the above sources in detail, it is deemed safer to examine the results of the operations of the Chicago & North-Western Railway, within the State of Illinois, as reported by the Railroad Commissioners, including the Iowa and Galena Divisions.

As I have already stated the population of the counties through which these lines pass, I now give the average per mile on the Iowa Division, 3,507; Galena Division, 2,822; Chicago & Pacific, 3,560. Omitting Cook and Du Page counties the average will be: Iowa Division, 1,146; Galena Division, 1,069; Chicago & Pacific, 1,087.

The earnings of the Chicago & North-Western Railroad, as reported by the Railroad Commissioners of the State of Illinois, was, for 1872, $7,600 per mile. Now, allowing that the earnings of the Chicago & Pacific Railroad will be two-thirds of this amount, we have $5,066, and deducting 60 per cent. for the cost of operating, $3,039, will leave $2,027, a net amount sufficient to pay 7 per cent. on $29,000 per mile of the road.

I refer to the fact that the Chicago & Pacific Railroad has advantages which have not in my knowledge been surpassed by any other new line of road in the country, viz.: the section through which it passes being rapidly developed in a high state of cultivation, and prepared to furnish a large amount of business for the road as fast as we reach it, and not being compelled to wait five to seven years for the country to become populated and business created.

The through connections will ensure a large and paying business, the local traffic on our Western roads being from 70 to 90 per cent. of the total earnings. For the above reasons it may be inferred with confidence that the Chicago & Pacific, when completed, will equal in its gross earnings the Chicago & North-Western Railway, say $8,000 per mile.

Respectfully submitted,

J. M. WHITMAN,

Chief Engineer.

Chicago, May 26th, 1873.

WILL THE ROAD PAY?

This is a question which each man who may think of investing in the bonds of the Chicago and Pacific Railroad Company will naturally ask: and upon the answer to it will depend his action. A glance at the map of the country through which the road passes, and the connections which it will make, will convince any person at all conversant with the carrying business of the great States of Illinois, Iowa, Wisconsin and Minnesota, that a railroad having its eastern terminus at Chicago, which is not only the metropolis of the Northwest, but also the center of the railway system of America, and running west, on almost an air line, through a rich and thickly settled country, studded with thriving villages and towns, and having for its western terminus the Mississippi river, that great artery of commerce in the west, *must and will pay.*

It has long been considered by American investors in railway securities, that any road running through a well settled country, and having its terminus in Chicago, will, from the very nature of things, do a paying business.

The first rail of the Chicago and Pacific Railroad was laid on the 10th day of July, 1872, and by the first of June, 1873, it will be completed to Elgin.

On the Division from Elgin west, work will be commenced at once, and pushed vigorously to rapid completion.

The first regular trains commenced running April 14th, 1873; and already a fine local business is being done.

It should be borne in mind that the Chicago and Pacific will not have to depend upon through business — obtained by expensive competition with other roads — for its income. While it will, without doubt, carry its full share of the products of Iowa, Wisconsin, Minnesota and the great Northwest, which seek Chicago for a market, it will, at the same time, do the largest local business, in proportion to the number of miles operated, of any road in Illinois, with the exception of the Chicago, Burlington and Quincy and the Chicago and Alton railroads.

The rich country through which it passes, already under a high state of cultivation, and inhabited mainly by people from the middle and eastern States: the successful manufacturing towns which are reached by it: the immense quantities of grain and stock raised, in the country traversed by and contiguous to the road; the number of suburban towns now being built and to be built along its line: its connections with the coal fields of central Illinois and Indiana on the south and east: its northern connections (by the way of Belvidere, Rockford and Warren) with the lumber and mineral regions of Wisconsin; its western connections at Forreston with the Illinois Central, at Shannon with the Western Union, and at Savanna with the Sabula, Ackley, and Dakota Railroad; its northern connection at Bellevue, Iowa, with the Dubuque and Minnesota Railroad, leading to St. Paul; the branches which will undoubtedly be built, giving it the business of several towns and a large tract of country now almost wholly devoid of railroad facilities, in addition to that which its main line reaches: its connections at Chicago with eastern and southern railroads, the Union Stock Yards and transfer privileges, which are very valuable; its large water-front and superior dock accommodations in Chicago — all go to warrant the assertion that THE CHICAGO AND PACIFIC RAILROAD WILL PAY.

www.ingramcontent.com/pod-product-compliance
Lightning Source LLC
Chambersburg PA
CBHW021558270326
41931CB00009B/1280
9783337257675

www.ingramcontent.com/pod-product-compliance
Lightning Source LLC
Chambersburg PA
CBHW021556270326
41931CB00009B/1247
* 9 7 8 3 3 3 7 2 9 6 8 6 5 *